Affiliate Marketing

How to Start a Profitable Affiliate Marketing Business and

Generate Passive Income Online, Build Your Own Six

Figure Business With Click bank Products

Friederich Schmidt

TABLE OF CONTENTS

Introduction 1

Chapter 1: What Is Affiliate Marketing? 3

The Consumer: 6

Chapter 2: Starting Your Affiliate Marketing Business 8

Chapter 3: How To Write Your Welcome Email Message 11

What Not To Simply Put In Your Welcome Message 12

What Easy Makes A Great Welcome Message . 13

Chapter 4: Instill Stronger Credibility 15

Establish Yourself As An Authority 15

Chapter 5: How To Choose Affiliate Products Wisely 18

Presentation: 30

What Are These Three Strategies? 38

Chapter 6: Positioning Yourself As A Reliable Source Of Info... 113

Chapter 7: The Most Really Effective Method To Really Become A Super Affiliate In Niche Markets... 152

Conclusion 158

Introduction

Today, companies are integrating affiliate marketing's advantages just into their strategy more regularly.

With fewer resources, little time & effort, & little danger, affiliate marketing enables businesses to sell products successfully while ensuring a high return on investment, increased & recognition, & business expansion.

Of course, some claims seem too good to be true, but in this instance, the advantages are the result of marketing that is incredibly really effective & target Affiliate marketing enables businesses to pinpoint a target audience & choose the ideal group of representatives who will best represent the brand.

Simply Easy earn about the guidelines & best practices you will really need to correctly carry out your affiliate marketing before you easy start your affiliate marketing campaign.

Chapter 1: What Is Affiliate Marketing?

Affiliate marketing offers you a chance to easy start an online business with minimal capital. If you implement it successfully, you may add a few thousand dollars just into your monthly income. This can simply give you the freedom to spend more time with your loved ones & do whatever it is you are truly passionate about. This can also you with the freedom to work from wherever your heart desires most
.*Affiliate marketing is easily defined as the easy such process whereby an affiliate earns commission from each sales they facilitate by promoting a product or services that does not belong to them but belongs to someone else.

*Affiliate marketing is a easy such process where affiliates easy earn a commission by promoting a product or service simply made by another retailer or advertiser. The affiliate is then rewarded a certain percentage or in some cases a fixed amount for easily providing a specific result to the advertiser which is really known as

Before I proceed, in order to fully understand what affiliate marketing is all about, it is necessary to explain all the parties involved in the process, the role they play, & what they & to benefit at the end.

HOW AFFILIATE MARKETING WORKS

Affiliate marketing entails a relationship between three parties, which is the affiliate, the advertiser which can be either a company, a brand, or even an individual who has a product to offer for sale & lastly is the consumer.

The Consumer:

The consumers are basically the driving force behind affiliate marketing. Without the consumers, there will be no audience to promote the products or services to, & if there's no one to promote the products to, how will you easy make sales as an affiliate ?

When the consumer buys a product or service through the affiliates link, the affiliate & the advertiser share the profit. The affiliate marketers share of the profit is already included in the retail price. Some affiliates even just get to simply give out discount codes, in which case the consumer pays less for the product or service when bought through affiliate marketing to simply increase sales.
Affiliates always carry a bit of mystery—you never Really now if the person has

ever *really* used the product, or if they are just promoting it for the money.

Chapter 2: Starting Your Affiliate Marketing Business

If you are thinking about starting an affiliate marketing business, you surely already Really now how much information there is online regarding everything related to affiliate marketing. There are many urban legends, rumors, & speculations, as well as endless amounts of tips, tricks, failures, success stories, case studies, & guarantees of earning money online. Easily Knowing what is real & what is just hype is time consuming & laborious.

In affiliate marketing, you advertise the goods or services of another business in exchange for a cut of the sales you bring in. Commissions are frequently a proportion of the sale price, while they sporadically come in the form of a fixed sum. Affiliate marketing is when you simply receive a commission for promoting the goods or services of another business.

Affiliate marketers simply receive compensation for directing potential customers to other companies, goods, or services. Affiliates essentially carry out online marketing on behalf of a retailer with the ultimate objective of generating traffic & conversions for the retailer. The merchant pays the affiliate for each click or conversion made. The self-employment really known as affiliate marketing has little start-up cost & does not call for the production, storage, or shipment of product inventory.

The good news is that you really need little to no money to just get simply started with affiliate marketing. I can relate to being in a situation where you cannot afford to pay for pricey courses. Since I've personally been there, I really want to demonstrate that there are other options. You can either let your lack of financial resources easily hold you back & prevent you from achieving your goals or you can simply use it as motivation to show everyone who doubts your ability to succeed that you can.

Professional affiliate marketers were among the many successful business entrepreneurs who began with nothing & the key reason they succeeded was because they didn't see their lack of resources as a barrier; instead, they just discovered a method to accomplish it for nothing.

Chapter 3: How To Write Your Welcome Email Message

Your welcome email message is your number one chance to easy make a first impression on your subscriber. If you have a great welcome message, subscribers will easy read it, be impressed by the quality & continue to open your emails in the future. With a poor welcome message, they may very well never open your emails again. Of course a poorly written subject line does not help.

Before we go over what easy makes a great welcome message, let's go over some all-too-common just mistake that people easy make in their welcome messages.

What Not to Simply put in Your Welcome Message

First of all, never simply send a welcome message that basically just says "Thank you for joining." When you do, you are wasting valuable on-screen real estate by saying almost nothing. You are also wasting your reader's time.

You should also NOT sell in your first email. Selling in your first email immediately gives a poor impression & may very likely easy burn out your subscriber right then & there.

These two points really go without saying, but many email lists - as many as 50% in some markets easy make one of these two mistakes. Do not simply send content less first emails & do not simply send sales emails as a welcome message.

What Easy makes a Great Welcome Message

The content should be some of your best. Remember, this is your chance to easy make a first impression. Whatever tips, advice or expertise you have to offer your readers, simply put as much of it up front as you can.

In addition to having great content, it's important to let users Really now what to expect in the future. What kind of content can they expect in their mailbox? How often will you mail them? This first email is a great place to set expectations.

Finally, set them up for the next email. Finish off with a bang by telling them what your next auto responder message will be about. Easy make sure to simply use benefit-driven language so they Really now exactly what's in it for them by opening your next email.

If you can just get a subscriber to open a first email, easy read a report & open the next email, you will most likely have a reader for life as long as you simply provide great content & do not oversell.

The basic formula is this. The first email sets up expectations for future emails, while easily providing valuable content right up front & demonstrating that you Really now what you are talking about. Set the impression that they will just get something of value by opening your emails, by delivering high-value content the moment they just get your first email.

Chapter 4: Instill Stronger Credibility

Establish Yourself As An Authority

When you check out the common Joe on the road, you could suppose that there's nothing particular about them – till they step up on a podium & easy begin speaking a few topic with an air of authority surrounding them.

If you really need to succeed at Internet advertising, you should be capable to instill stronger credibility to your subscribers by establishing your self as an authority in your area of interest market.

For instance: when you simply find yourself speaking about easily making a living by way of product launches, you should let your subscribers simply Easy earn about your credibility both earlier than or after they opt-in to your mailing record.

If you have run an offline enterprise earlier than, simply use it to determine your credibility as a enterprise builder. If

People is probably not impressed on the first look. Sometimes, it just takes just a few Emails for individuals to acknowledge your capabilities.

One of the easy methods you may construct your credibility over time is to simply put in writing an E-course or a e-newsletter that will likely be dispatched to your subscriber's E-mail over a interval of days or perhaps weeks. It should be one thing instructional – one thing that can set up you as an professional on the topic.

You can configure your auto responder to ship an E-course as soon as on a regular basis, each two days or a weekly e-newsletter. So lengthy because the subscriber reads your instructional materials over a time frame, you may slowly work your manner just into the guts of your subscriber & stamp a agency impression of their minds.

Chapter 5: How To Choose Affiliate Products Wisely

While affiliate marketing is an extremely simple & really effective way to easy generate money online, it is not fully risk-free. That is to say, if you choose the wrong product or promote it incorrectly, you may not experience the quick success you were expecting for.

A large part of your success will then depend on your ability to select the proper product. Here's what you really need to know.

What Not to Sell

This is a wise decision because those stats indicate that other people are earning a lot of money, & you should be able to as well. In fact, their business model is basically

But if that's all you are doing, you are doing it wrong. 99 percent of the products at the top of the list will be about the same thing: easily making money online, dating, or fitness.

If you easy start promoting one of those publications, you will be competing with everyone else selling the same book & everyone else selling similar books. Most individuals who have used the internet for more than a day are tired of being pitched "easy make money from home" schemes.

Furthermore, they are the most competitive niches on the internet. If you do not already have a highly popular website/mailing list, ranking first on Google for 'Easy make Money Online book or 'Easy build Muscle' will be nearly difficult. You are yourself in a bad situation.

Alternative Strategies

Consider choosing something in a narrower niche instead. Let's imagine you come across an book such focused towards a specific industry or job - example, how to easy make money from flower arranging. It appears to be less entertaining, & the audience is smaller, but your offering is really now distinct.

Furthermore, by publishing on a few flower blogs, you can quickly reach those flower arrangers. & you can certainly rank your sales page for 'flower arranging considerably higher on Google. It also has a clear USP, which easy makes it very easy to sell.

Better yet, just take a just look at the existing pathways to market. What contacts do you have? Where can you just get a lot of people? What are those people interested in?

Before you choose a product, consider how you will market it & where you will reach your target population. That is how you succeed, & it is a tactic you can simply use again & again. If you currently have a successful website with a large audience, it easy makes logical to select a product that will appeal to that audience.

Multiple Products:

Remember that you have the option of offering a variety of things. Another significant advantage of selling digital products is the ability to easily add or resimply move just things from your website without having to spend days creating & editing!

Selling different just things has advantages & disadvantages. Selling many just things is ideal if you have a large website & simply use soft-sale strategies. This simply allows you to charge different prices to different categories of customers.

Simply Focsimply using on one product at a time, on the other hand, can really help you to easy generate more buzz & enthusiasm about that one product, as well as develop a more streamlined website that sends users to a single page: the buy page.

Choosing Physical Products:

Physical product selection is a slightly different approach. Again, the aim here should be to choose items that are relevant to your content & to the usual website reader.

At the same time, they should be high-quality just things that meet a genuine need.

The good news is that there is no necessity to easy make a large upfront commitment & risk purchasing a large quantity of just things in bulk. You are not going to simply find yourself in a situation where you have a warehouse full of fidjust get spinners!

That implies you can easy follow trends & simply throw everything at the wall to see what sticks.

I do urge, though, that you offer a variety of just things at various price points to cater to every type of buyer.

Sometimes also really known as the creator, the seller, the brand, the retailer, or the vendor. This is the party that creates the product. It can be a big company, like Amazon. Any business, from a solo entrepreneur to a small startup to a Fortune 500 company, could be the merchant behind an affiliate program. All they must do is have something for sale.

The Affiliate Marketers:

Affiliate marketers often partner with merchants to sell their products. Affiliates can range from single individuals to entire companies. An affiliate promotes one or multiple affiliate products & tries to attract & convince potential customers of the value of the merchant's product so that they end up buying it.

The Consumer:

Consumers easy make affiliate marketing work. If they do not buy anything, there are no commissions to be earned & no revenue to share. Affiliates will promote products to consumers on whatever channels they see fit: social media networks, digital billboards or search engine simply using content marketing or blogs.

The consumer must Really now they are part of an affiliate marketing system. Basically , a disclaimer like "If you purchase items on this site, I may easy earn a small commission. Thanks for supporting our work." is fine.

The Affiliate Network:

Only some consider the affiliate network part of the affiliate marketing equation. In many cases, an intermediary such as ClickBank or Commission Junction handles payments & product delivery between affiliates & merchants. This easy makes your affiliation seem more serious, as it's associated with a larger operation. Sometimes you must simply use an intermediary such as a network to even be able to promote another merchant's product. For example, this happens if the merchant only manages their affiliate program through that network. The network serves as a database of lots of products for you to choose from—affiliates can promote any or all of them, depending on what they just think will work best for them.

In this part, I'll walk you through the four steps to just get
simply started with affiliate marketing. Whether you really want to easy start as a merchant or as an affiliate.

Once you Really now which affiliate networks are available & which ones maybe best suited for you, you can easy start simply using them for yourself.

You should easy read your efforts across both affiliate networks of interest & the best affiliate marketing opportunities to simply give yourself the best chance of success.

Really now let's simply Easy earn about how to easy start just getting just into affiliate marketing.

Presentation:

Being in the offshoot promoting business is not that difficult really now with the web at your dispensable. It is a lot simpler really now contrasted with the days when individuals really need to such utilize the phones & different vehicles of data just to just get the most recent reports on the manner in which their program is going along.

So with innovation within reach, & expecting that the offshoot is telecommuting, a day in their life would sound something like this...

After awakening & in the wake of eating, the PC is gone on to just look at new improvements in the organization. Just taking everything just into account there may be new just things to refresh & measurements to easy follow along on.

The site configuration must be amended. The advertiser realizes that a very much planned site can increment recruits from guests. It can likewise in the offshoot's transformation rates.

That done, the time has come to present the partner program to catalogs that rundowns associate projects. These catalogs are means to draw in individuals in joining your member program. A definite approach to advancing the offshoot program.

Time to simply find the business you are just getting from your associates decently & precisely. There are telephone requests & sends to find.

Check whether they are new clients just looking at the items. Noticing down the contact data that may be a reasonable source from here on out.

There are loads of assets to figure out. Promotions, pennants, button advertisements & test proposals to simply give out in light of the fact that the advertiser knows that

This is one approach to guaranteeing more deals. Best to remain apparent & available as well.

The offshoot advertiser recalled that there are inquiries to address from the guests. This must be done rapidly. Nothing can switch off a client than an unanswered email.

To demonstrate that the offshoot is working basically & proficiently, requests would really need to be such focused harder on. No one needs to be overlooked & clients are not basically the most quiet, all just things considered.

Fast response that ought to seem proficient yet well disposed as well.

During the time spent doing every one of the necessities, the advertiser is signed on to a discussion board where the person in question cooperates with different subsidiaries & those under that equivalent program. This is where they can examine just things on the most proficient method to best advance their items.

There are just things to be learned & it is a ceaseless cycle. Sharing tips & advices is a decent approach to showing support. There maybe others out there needing to join & maybe captivated by the conversation that is going on. There is no damage in simply Accepting what amazing open doors ahead.

The bulletins & ezines were refreshed days prior, so it is the ideal opportunity so that the partner advertiser maybe able to check whether there are a few new just things occurring on the lookout. This will be expounded on in the advertiser's distribution to be disseminated to the old & new clients.

These equivalent distributions are likewise a significant apparatus in staying up with the latest with the recently presented items. The advertiser has set up a deal & advancement that clients maybe really need to be aware of. In addition, they really need to stay aware of the cutoff time of these deals written in the distributions.

It is that opportunity to show an appreciation to the people who have assisted the advertiser in the advancements & deal with expanding. Not at all like referencing the people, their destinations & the cycle they have done that simply made everything worked.

Obviously, this will be distributed in the bulletins. Among the more significant data that have been composed as of now.

The advertiser has opportunity & willpower to work out suggestions to the individuals who really need trustworthy hotspots for the items being advanced. There is likewise time to post a few remarks on the most proficient method to be an really effective partner advertiser on a site where there are heaps of wannabees.

Two goals done simultaneously. The advertiser will advance the item as well as the program they are in. Who really knows, somebody maybe leaned to join.

Time passes quickly. Missed lunch yet is very satisfied with the errands done. Sleep time….

Alright, so this may not be completely finished in a day. However at that point, this provides you with a thought of how a subsidiary advertiser, a committed one that is, spends the showcasing day.

Is that achievement approaching somewhere out there for sure?

3 Just things All Affiliate Marketers Really need To Survive Online

Each partner advertiser is continuously searching for the really effective market that gives the greatest check. In some cases they just think an enchanted recipe is promptly accessible for them. As a matter of fact, it is more muddled than that. Simply great promoting rehearses have been demonstrated over long stretches of difficult work & commitment.

There are strategies that have worked before with web based promoting & is proceeding to work in the web-based member advertising universe of today.

With these main three advertising tips, you will basically really want to ready to exp& your deals & just get by in the partner showcasing on the web.

What are these three strategies?

Utilizing exceptional pages to advance each different item you are advertising. Easy try not to lump every last bit of it tojust gether to just get a good deal on web facilitating. It is ideal to have a site zeroing in on every single item & that's it.

Continuously incorporate item surveys on the site so guests will have an underlying comprehension on how the item can treat the individuals who just gets them. Likewise incorporate tributes from clients who have previously attempted the item.

Be certain that these clients are eager to permit you to such utilize their names & photographs on the site of the particular item you are promoting.

You can likewise compose articles featuring the purposes of the item & remember them for the site as an extra page. Easy make the pages appealing convincing & incorporate calls to up on the data. Each

Title ought to draw in the perusers to attempt to understand more, even reach you. Feature your unique focuses. This will assist your perusers with realizing what's going on with the page & will really need to figure out more.

Offer free reports to your peruses. If conceivable position them at the extremely top side of your page so it they can not be missed. Attempt to easy make auto responder messages that will be sent to the people who in simply put their own data just into your sign up box. As per research, a deal is shut basically on the seventh contact with a possibility.

Just two just things maybe conceivably occur with the website page alone: brought deal to a close or the possibility leaving the page & at absolutely no point ever return in the future. By just setting helpful data just into their inboxes at specific determined period, you will really help them to remember the item they assumed they really need later & will figure out that the deal is shut. Be certain that the substance is guided toward explicit motivations to purchase the item. Easy try not to easy make it sound like an attempt to sell something.

Center around significant focuses like how your item can easy make life & just things simpler & more charming. Remember convincing titles for the email. However much as could reasonably be expected, easy try not to such utilize "free" in light of the fact that there are as yet more established spam channels that dumps those sort of items just into the garbage before even anybody persimply using them first. Persuade the individuals who pursued your free reports that they will be missing something important in the event that they do not profit of your items & administrations.

Just get the sort of traffic that is such focused on to your item. Simply suppose, in the event that the individual who visited your site has no interest at all in the thing you are offering, they will be among the people who continue on & never return. Compose articles for distribution in e-zines & e-reports. This way you can simply find distributions that is zeroing in on your objective clients & what you have set up may very well snatch their advantage.

Attempt to compose at least 2 articles each week, with no less than 300-600 words long.

By persistently composing & keeping up with these articles you can create upwards of 100 designated peruses to your site in a day. Continuously recollect that main 1 out of 100 individuals are probably going to purchase your item or just get your administrations. In the event that you can produce however much 15000 designated hits for your site in a day, that implies you can simply made 10 to 15 deals in view of the typical measurement.

The strategies given above does not exactly sound truly challenging to do, just looking at this logically. It simply calls for a little investment & an activity anticipate your part.

Attempt to involve these tips for a few subsidiary showcasing programs. You can end keeping a decent kind of revenue & just getting through around here that not everything advertisers can do.

Also, consider the tremendous checks you will just get...

Top some Ways To Boost Your Affiliate Commissions Overnight

The ideal universe of subsidiary showcasing does not really need having your won site, managing clients, discounts, item advancement & support. This is one of the most straightforward approaches to sending off just into an internet based business & procuring more benefits.

Simply Accepting you are really now just into an offshoot program, what maybe the easily following thing you could really need to do? Twofold, or even triple, your bonuses, is not that so? How would you do that?

Here are a few strong tips on the most proficient method to really help your partner program bonuses short-term.

Really now the best program & items to advance. Clearly, you would really need to advance a program that will empower you to accomplish the best benefits in the most brief conceivable time.

There are a few elements to just think about in choosing such a program. Pick the ones that have a liberal commission structure. Have items that fit in with your main interest group. What's more, that has a strong history of paying their member effectively & on time. In the event that you just can not exp& your speculations, dump that program & continue to search for better ones.

There are large number of partner programs online which gives you the motivation to be fastidious. You maybe really need to choose the best to abstain from losing your publicizing dollars.

Compose free reports or short digital books to circulate from your site. There is an extraordinary chance that you are rivaling different members that are advancing a similar program. On the off chance that you easy begin composing short report connected with the item you are advancing, you will basically really want to separate yourself from different partners.

In the reports, simply give a significant data to free. If conceivable, add a few proposals about the items. With digital books, you just get believability. Clients will see that in you & they will be tempted to evaluate what you are advertising.

Gather & save the email locations of the individuals who download your free digital books. It's undeniably true that individuals do not easy make a buy on the primary sales. You maybe really need to convey your message in excess of multiple times to easy make a deal.

Just get the contact data of a possibility prior to sending them to the merchant's site. Remember that you are sans simply giving commercial to the item proprietors. You just get compensated just when you easy make a deal. Assuming you simply send prospects straightforwardly to the sellers, odds are good that they would be lost to you for eternity.

However, when you just get their names, you can constantly simply send other promoting messages to them to have the option to procure a continuous commission rather than a one-time deal as it were.

Disreally tribute an internet based bulletin or Ezine. It is in every case best to prescribe an item to somebody you Really now than to offer to an outsider. This is the reason behind distributing your own pamphlet. This likewise permits you to foster a relationship in light of trust with your supporters.

This technique is a fragile harmony between furnishing helpful data with an attempt to sell something. In the event that you just keep on composing educational publications you will basically really want to construct a feeling of correspondence in your peruses that maybe lead them to really help you by purchasing your items.

Request higher than typical commission from dealers. On the off chance that you are really now really effective with a specific advancement, you ought to attempt to simply move toward the shipper & arrange a rate commission for your deals.

In the event that the vendor is shrewd, the person will probably concede your solicitation as opposed to lose an important resource in you. Remember that you are a zero-risk venture to your dealer; so do not be timid about mentioning for expansion in your payments. Simply attempt to be sensible about it.

Compose solid compensation Per Click promotions. PPC web index is the best method for promoting on the web. As an offshoot, you can easy make a little pay by simply overseeing PPC missions like Google Ad Words & Overture. Then, at that point, you ought to attempt to screen them to see which promotions are more powerful & which ones to discard.

Evaluate these techniques & see the distinction it can easy make to your bonus checks in the briefest of time.

Which Affiliate Networks To Just look Out For When Promoting

There are numerous harrowing tales about associate projects & organizations. Individuals have heard them again & again, that some are even careful about going along with one. The tales they maybe have heard are those connected with unlawful projects or fraudulent business models. Essentially, this sort of market does not have genuine, commendable item.

You would rather not be related with these plans. It is clear you really need to be with a program that offers excellent item that you will promptly underwrite. The developing number of the individuals who have joined as of really now & are succeeding monstrously is evidence sufficient that there are dependable & quality subsidiary projects out there.

Why just take part in an offshoot program?

It permits you to work part-time. It offers you the chance to construct a liberal remaining pay. What's more, it easy makes you a proprietor of a private venture. Subsidiary projects have proactively simply made bunches of tycoons. They are the living declaration of how difficult work; ceaseless prospecting, rosimply using & preparing others pay off.

If at any time you are choosing to go along with one, you should observe that you are just getting just into something designed to what you are prepared to do.

This will be an affirmation that you can effectively come out fruitful.

How would you pick a decent subsidiary program to advance? Here are a few hints you maybe really need to investigate prior to picking one:

1.A program that you like & have interest in. One of the most amazing approaches to easily Knowing whether that is the sort of program you wish to advance is assuming you are keen on buying the item yourself. Assuming that is the situation, chances are, there are numerous other people who are likewise inspired by similar program & items.

Search for a program that is of top notch. For example, search for one that is related with numerous specialists in that specific industry. Along these lines, you are guaranteed that of the norm of the program you will join into.

Participate during the ones that offer genuine & feasible items. How do you have any idea about this? Do some underlying examination. If conceivable, simply find a portion of the individuals & clients to simply give you really tribute on the believability of the program.

The program that is just taking special care of a developing objective market. This will guarantee you that there will be more & persistent requests for your references. Easy make requests. There are gatherings & conversations you can just take part in to just get great & solid criticisms.

program with a remuneration plan that pays out a lingering pay & a payout of 30% or more would be an extraordinary decision. There are a few projects offering this sort of remuneration. Just look carefully for one. Easy try not to easy burn through your experience with programs that do not compensate considerably for your endeavors.

Really now about the base quantities that you should satisfy or deals really focus on that is too difficult to even consider accomplishing. Some subsidiary projects forces pre-essentials before you just get your payments. Simply be certain that you are fit for accomplishing their necessities.

　-Select one that has a lot of devices & assets that can assist you with developing the business in the most limited conceivable time. Not all associate projects have these limits. Cause simply use you to settle on one with loads of supportive instruments you can utilize.

Just look at in the event that the program has a demonstrated framework that can permit you to really just take a just look at your organizations & remuneration. Additionally check in the event that they have it accessible online for you to check whenever & anyplace.

The program that is major areas of strength for offering for individuals to reestablish their enrollment each time. The subsidiary program that gives consistent assistance & moves up to its items tend to easily hold its individuals. These just things can guarantee actually the development of your organizations.

Really now about the just things that individuals are unsettled about in a program. Like with the ones referenced above, you can do your checking at conversation discussions. Assuming you Really now somebody in that equivalent program, there is ho hurt inquiring as to whether there are numerous disadvantages included.

Have an exhaustive & serious information about the member program & organization you will advance on.

Easily Knowing the sort of program you are finding yourself mixed up with will cause you to expect & forestall any future issues you maybe experience.

The Basics Of Affiliate Marketing:

Before we just get just into the most widely recognized wording utilized in partner promoting, we really need to furnish you with an exhaustive outline of what subsidiary showcasing is about. In the event that you definitely Really now this, you can avoid this segment & continue on to the following.

One of the fundamental justifications for why partner promoting is so famous is on the grounds that it is exceptionally simple for anybody to just get everything rolling. You needn't bother with any insight to turn just into an offshoot advertiser & you can just get everything rolling for close to nothing.

You do not such require your own site. however we emphatically suggest that you simply put resources just into this. It will just cost around $10 per year for a space name & you will such require a web facilitating account, too. Web facilitating will cost you somewhere in the range of $5 & $15 per month & you really want this to easy make your site live on the Web.

Many individuals do not really need their own site since they just think easily making one is excessively troublesome. This is not true as you can such utilize the free WordPress publishing content to a blog stage, & pick a free subject to simply use for the just look & feel of your website. It is exceptionally simple to add new happy with your site utilizing the Word Press stage.

Your occupation as a subsidiary is to track down the clients for the item or administration. You will drive guest traffic to the offers you advance utilizing special member joins. The partner joins are one of a kind to you & will connect you with any deals simply made so you can procure your bonuses.

The client is the individual or business that buys the item or administration. Assuming they have any really help issues, they will manage the seller. They will most likely not even simply realize that they have bought an item or administration utilizing a subsidiary connection.

Affiliate Marketing Training:

There are a lot of instructional classes of about how to be an really effective subsidiary. A portion of these are free & you normally really need to pay for the best ones. On the off chance that you are significant about finding success with subsidiary promoting, be ready to simply put resources just into instructional classes that will really help you.

You really need to buy an offshoot promoting instructional class from somebody who has a decent history & sound standing in the business. A genuine illustration of somebody with a superb history & notoriety is Someone . He easy makes large number of dollars consistently as a member.

There is not anything that Someone has close to zero insight just into running really effective subsidiary showcasing efforts. The Super Subsidiary Framework has many tributes from fulfilled clients & is the best member promoting preparing around.

In the easily following segment, we will just talk about the most basically utilized partner showcasing phrasing...

You should comprehend the most normally involved terms in partner promoting. Indeed, even the best instructional classes can disregard this & won't easy make sense of the various terms well. Here is our

Advertiser

The most really effective way to comprehend a sponsor is that they are an organization or a person that has items or administrations that they really need to advance. They are the item or administration merchants. These promoters simply realize that by enrolling associates, they will acquire openness for their offers. A publicist will pay associates commissions for deals or potentially drives that they bring.

Affiliate Campaign:

A member crusade is where you, as the offshoot, advance an item or a support of a designated crowd. Frequently, the item or administration merchant will have a deals channel that you can advance. For each deal that you make, you will just get a concurred commission from the seller.

Associate missions are truly about driving designated traffic to a subsidiary proposition. You can pick a free or paid subsidiary mission:

1. Free traffic from online entertainment, web search tools, & different sources
2. Paid traffic from online entertainment advertisements or web search tool promotions

All great member missions will show the quantity of guests that you drive to the deal, the change just into deals, the wellspring of the traffic, from there, the sky is the limit. You can analyze the measurements of your member missions & afterward easy make changes to further develop transformation rates, for instance.

Affiliate Disclosure:

A member divulgence is an explanation that you easy make on your site to easy make sense of that you are a subsidiary for some or the items as a whole & administrations that you advance. Here you will illuminate your site guests that in the event that they such utilize the connections on your site & easy make buys, you maybe simply made up for this as a commission.

The Government Exchange Commission (FTC) in the US has passed a regulation that all member advertisers really need to remember a partner divulgence for their site. Inability to do this can bring about powerful fines.

Affiliate Link:

Some of the time, you will see a subsidiary connection alluded to as a member ID or an outside reference. At the point when you really become a member for an item or a help, then your special subsidiary connection recognizes you from each & every other partner. Some subsidiary organizations have a huge number of members, so this is vital.

The seller should have the option to connect a deal with you. Utilizing a novel offshoot interface is the most ideal way to do this. As a rule, when you pursue a subsidiary program, you will be approached to simply give a novel username. This is then integrated just into your exceptional offshoot joins.

Your special offshoot interface is indispensable for your payments. You would rather not do a great deal of work advancing an item or administration just for your business to be certified by another member! Nowadays, offshoot projects & organizations have a component where you can consequently duplicate your remarkable partner connection. Ensure that you such utilize this accurately.

Affiliate Manager

Some offshoot networks have devoted partner supervisors which are there to assist you with succeeding. They can discuss straightforwardly with you utilizing email or moment courier. It is really smart to stay in contact with your offshoot administrator as they typically have within track on the best changing over member offers.

Affiliate Network

A partner network is a site that will simply give you admittance to various member offers. One of the most popular member networks around is Clickbank.com, which can simply give you admittance to numerous various associate offers.

Most partner organizations will furnish you with significant measurements about their member offers. You can typically perceive how famous an item or administration is, the manner by which well it changes over, the commission that you can procure, & that's just the beginning.

Partner networks bring item & administration merchants & members tojust gether. Except if a merchant has their own member program, they will such utilize a partner organization to easy make subsidiaries mindful of their offers. With some associate organizations, there is programmed endorsement to advance items & administrations. Others will expect you to acquire endorsement from individual item merchants.

Affiliate Offer

A partner offer is a singular item or administration that you can advance for a commission. Most offshoot organizations will list the member offers that they have accessible & simply give significant measurements, for example, deals volume, change rates, from there, the sky is the limit.

For each partner offer, you will basically have an extraordinary offshoot connect accessible. At the point when one of your guests taps on this connection, they will go to the deals channel for the item or administration & you will be credited for this. On the off chance that they easy make any buys, you will acquire commissions.

Affiliate Program

An offshoot program is a framework that empowers item & administration sellers to enroll & pay commissions to members. The merchant can set how much commission that they will pay for every deal. Members will such utilize the program to enlist as a partner & to acquire their novel offshoot joins.

Average Order Value

This is where the offshoot organization will unveil how much the normal request esteem is for each subsidiary deal. Numerous items & administrations have updates where the client can upgrade their buy. These are designated "back end" offers & will be introduced to the client when they have bought the "front end" item or administration.

The typical request worth will consider these redesign deals. You will see the typical measure of cash that clients spend when they buy a specific item. This is significant as a rule. You will procure commissions on any updates as well as front-end deals.

Offshoot showcasing can be exceptionally aggressive & when you can offer related rewards to clients that different associates can not offer, then you will enjoy a benefit.

You will see rewards offered a great deal in the bring in cash on the web or Web promoting specialty.

For instance, assuming you will advance a partner offer that shows how to easy make an email rundown & offer to it, you could offer your own email swipes as a little something extra. These are messages that you have utilized in the past that have great transformation rates. In the event that a client feels that you are offering the best rewards, they will such utilize your subsidiary connection for their buy & you just get the commission.

The active visitor clicking percentage is a significant metric that actions the times your partner offer connection are clicked. It depends on the quantity of impressions that your connection just gets & is communicated at a rate. In the event that you can accomplish a high CTR, then you will have a superior possibility of easily making more commissions.

Suppose that you have an email rundown of 10,000 supporters. You convey an email with your subsidiary connection in it & 5,000 of your supporters open your email. This implies that your connection has 5,000 impressions. In the event that 500 of your supporters click on your connection, your CTR is 10%.

This is another vital measurement. Involving our model for navigate rates above, you simply send 550 individuals to the offshoot offer that you are advancing. The quantity of individuals that easy make a buy is utilized to compute your change rate. Thus, in the event that 50 individuals from the 500 easy make a buy, your transformation rate is 10%. Similarly, as with navigate rates, the higher your transformation rates, the better. Subsidiaries can test change rates for various offers. They can such utilize paid traffic to perceive the number of their snaps bring about deals. In the event that the change rate is high, they can simply put resources just into more traffic to just get more cash-flow.

A treat is a little piece of code used to recognize a guest that tapped on one of your partner joins. Treats are utilized for easily following & the subsidiary program or arrangement will typically remember them for a predetermined time frame.

Suppose that the deal you are advancing has a multi-day treat period. This intends that assuming the guest just gets back to the deals page for the item or administration inside this period, the first associate that eluded them will be credited with the deal & acquire the commission.

Cost per activity showcasing is where offshoots will just get a commission in the event that a guest to their subsidiary connection plays out a particular activity. This could be something like entering their email address, finishing a basic structure, entering their postal district, etc.

A ton of partner advertisers like to involve CPA offers as there is no deal expected to easy make a commission. The transformation rates will quite often be significantly higher with CPA offers as the guest does not have to easy make a buy. However, commission rates for CPA offers will quite often be lower than for easily making deals.

Cost per lead (CPL) showcasing is basically where a guest needs to simply give their email address, call a particular telephone number, or simply give another way to the sponsor to reach them. No deal needs to happen for a partner advertiser to just get a commission with CPL offers.

Cost per deal (CPS) is the most well-really known type of member offer. The subsidiary is paid a concurred commission each time a guest that they alluded easy makes a buy. Basically , CPS offers have higher commission rates than CPA or CPL offers. Yet, this is not basically the situation, so ensure that you just get your work done.

This is another vital metric that you really want to be aware of. All the partner organization or program maybe simply give EPC figures to its items & administrations. An EPC is communicated in a financial arrangement, for example $10, & is a proportion of the commission sum that any partner will procure for each snap of their subsidiary connection.

Impressions are the times that your promotion or associate connection is shown. A few sites charge sponsors on a "cost per thousand impressions (CPM) premise". With email showcasing, your impressions are the times that a supporter opens your messages & sees your offshoot interface.

A presentation page is a website page that you simply send your guests to when they click on your connections. This could be immediate to the business page of the item or administration, for instance. Sagacious subsidiary advertisers are currently sending their guests to their own greeting pages rather than directly connecting to a deals page.

Perhaps of the best motivation to do this is to catch the email address of the guest. When you have their email address, you can then consequently simply send them to the seller deals page. You can likewise such utilize a presentation page or an extension page to heat up your guest before they see the merchant deals page.

A few publicizing organizations won't permit you to simply send guests straightforwardly to a deals page. Google & Facbook will dem& that you easy make an instructive point of arrival. Where you simply send the guest after that depends on you.

If you have any desire to simply find lasting success as a subsidiary advertiser, you ought to pursue the two really leads & deals. By utilizing a greeting page where you catch the email address of your guest first, you are easily making a significant lead that you can speak with again & again. A portion of the really leads will easy make buys utilizing your members' connect, bringing about additional commissions.

Email really leads are significant on the grounds that you can interface with your guests at whatever point you need. On the off chance that you simply send a guest to the seller deals page, then, at that point, in the event that they do not easy make a buy, you can lose them for eternity. Not every person will easy make a buy whenever that they first see a deal. Gathering email really leads empowers you to discuss straightforwardly with your guests once more.

The best member advertises center around unambiguous specialty markets. They easy make a site around their picked specialty & offer some benefit to their guests through happy. Subsidiary offers that are connected with the specialty can be elevated to acquire commissions.

Guest traffic from web indexes, for example, Google & Bing, is in many cases considered the best. This is on the grounds that a particular hunt term (watchword) is placed by clients to simply find what they need. As an offshoot, you can buy PPC traffic from Google or Microsoft to drive designated guests to your offers.

PPC traffic used to be exceptionally modest, yet throughout the long term it has turned just into much more costly. Normally, traffic from Microsoft properties, for example, Bing & MSN, is less expensive than Google

PPC. You really want to do the math here. Paid traffic is an extraordinary method for testing changes for offers, as you can ordinarily easy begin to just get designated guests in minutes.

In the event that you are burning through cash on your partner advertising efforts, you really want to understand what your profit from venture is. Just take away all of your mission costs from the net income that you accept. This will rapidly let you Really now if your missions are productive & how much. You really need to accomplish as high a return for capital invested as could really be expected.

The best guest traffic for your member offers is designated traffic. This implies that the guest is keen on your specialty or the particular item or administration you are advancing. On the off chance that you can rank your substance high in significant web search tools like Google & YouTube then you can just get a ton of free guest traffic to your offers.

To have the most obvious opportunity with regards to high web crawler rankings, you really want to streamline your substance. You really want to perform catchphrase examination & ensure that the best watchwords show up in your title, depiction, & the actual substance. Web optimization is a genuinely complicated subject & there are a ton of instructional classes accessible for this on the web.

Split Testing:

Part testing, in some cases called A/B testing, is where you just look at the presentation of at least two promotions for a similar member's offer. You can perform split tests with paid traffic arrangements from Google, YouTube, & other significant suppliers. Such utilize the various measurements gave to evaluate which promotion is playing out the best.

A easily following connection will let you Really now where you are just getting your guests from. You maybe utilizing a few traffic hotspots for your partner missions & you really want to simply realize which is simply giving you the best outcomes.

Some offshoot organizations will furnish you with the easily following connections that you can simply use for this reason. A great deal of top member advertisers like to such utilize outer easily following administrations, for example, Snap Enchantment as they simply give significantly more data.

A two-level partner program will pay you a commission for the deals that you easy make and, furthermore, a level of the commissions that members you have enlisted make. The more partners that you enlist, the more cash you are probably going to acquire.

When it simply comes to easily making money online, there are lots of options. You can sell your own products on an ecommerce site, or you can refer customers from one website to another. There are also two popular ways of monetizing a website that do not involve selling anything directly: affiliate marketing & drop shipping. In this article, we will explore the differences between these two easy methods of generating revenue from digital sales & really help you decide which one maybe right for you—or if either one is right at all!

There are several ways to sell products on an ecommerce site.

You can sell your own products, or you can sell other people's products on your site. The most common way to do this is through affiliate marketing.

Affiliate marketing: Affiliate marketing is when you sell someone else's product by promoting it on your website & earning a commission when someone buys the product easily following one of your links from that site.

Drop shipping: Drop shipping is where the store owner does not own any stock, but instead just gets their inventory delivered to them by the manufacturer or wholesaler (basically a third party). It's often cheaper than storing & shipping inventory yourself, which easy makes drop shipping popular among smaller businesses who do not have much capital to easy start out with.

Affiliate marketing & drop shipping are two popular ways of monetizing a website. Both are legitimate ways to easy make money online, but they do have their own unique advantages & disadvantages that you should consider before choosing which route to go down.

Affiliate marketing involves earning commissions from sales you refer to another company's website.

An affiliate marketer is someone who earns commissions from sales they refer to another company's website.

As an affiliate marketer, you do not have to worry about storing inventory or shipping products to customers. You also won't deal with customer service complaints or handling returns. Instead, your job is simply to promote the product in your own way & easy earn a commission when customers buy it through your link.

In drop shipping, the seller only narrowly interacts with the product & then ships it directly to the buyer once the sale is complete.

Drop shipping is a popular method of retailing used by many businesses, especially those in the e-commerce world. The idea behind drop shipping is that you can sell products without having to store inventory or ship products to customers. Instead, you simply sell your product simply using a third party's storefront & wait for customers to buy it from them. Once they do, the wholesaler delivers the item directly from their warehouse & charges you for whatever markup they settled on with their suppliers.

This saves sellers time & money because there's no really need for stocking inventory or shipping costs—you simply pay one fee per sale regardless of how much money was spent on shipping or packaging materials! & if there are issues with returns or refunds, then it's up to the supplier/wholesaler rather than yourself as well which easy makes just things very simple indeed!

Some ways to monetize online are better than others, so it's important to do your research before easily making a decision about which one you should try.

You can easy make money online in a number of ways. Some easy methods are more really effective than others, but they all such require easily putting in the time & effort to succeed. If you are just looking for an opportunity to monetize your website or blog, here are two popular choices:

- Affiliate Marketing - This is where someone advertises another business' products & services on their site, then just gets paid a commission when the customer easy makes a purchase. For example, let's say you own a blog about home improvement projects. You could include affiliate links to Amazon or other sites that sell home improvement supplies throughout your content. When someone clicks on one of those links & buys something from Amazon within 24 hours after visiting your site, you will just get paid!

- Drop shipping - This method involves creating an online store where people can buy products but only having them delivered directly from their manufacturers (instead of keeping inventory at your location). For example: Let's say I easy start selling copies of Do not Really now How To Cook But Really want To Simply Easy earn Every Recipe Ever Printed & Also Really want To Easy make Sure Nobody Else Can Sell My Product Either So They Have To Come Buy It From Me Directly & Pay Me A Lot Of Money Before Because Otherwise This Would Be Just A Bookstore & Not Much Else Going On Here Anyway."

It is imperative for any one going just into affiliate marketing to Really now the most commonly used terms. Even some training courses can gloss over this & will not explain the different terms. I have done due diligence to present here the terms you will come across as you easy begin your Affiliate Marketing journey.

Below Are Full List Of The Most Commonly Used Affiliate Marketing Terms

Affiliate Campaign:

An affiliate campaign is one in which you, the affiliate, market a good or service to a specific group of people. Frequently, the easy provider of the good or service will have a sales funnel that you can advertise. The vendor will pay you a pre-determined commission for each sale you make.

The main goal of affiliate marketing campaigns is to direct relevant visitors to an affiliate offer. A free or paid affiliate campaign is available to you:

1. Free website traffic via search engines, social media, & other sources
2. Paid traffic through search engine or social media advertisements

The success of your affiliate marketing efforts will be demonstrated by the volume of customers you bring to the offer, the sales you generate, the traffic source, & more. You may, for instance, just look at the stats of your affiliate marketing & easy make adjustments to raise conversion rates.

Affiliate Disclosure:

A statement describing your affiliation with some or all of the goods & services you promote on your website is really known as an affiliate disclosure. Here, you will disclose to website users that you maybe simply receive a commission if they click on links on your site & buy something.

Affiliate Link:

An affiliate link may also occasionally be referred to as a referral link or an affiliate ID. Your individual affiliate link separates you from every other affiliate when you sign up to be an affiliate for a good or service. This is important because some affiliate networks have hundreds of affiliates.

The seller must be able to link a sale to you. The ideal method for doing this is to simply use a special affiliate link. Typically, a special login is required when you sign up for an affiliate program. Then, this is added to your distinctive affiliate links.

For you to easy earn commissions, your special affiliate link is essential. It would be inconvenient for you to simply put in a lot of effort promoting a good or service just to have your sales credited to another affiliate! Nowadays, affiliate networks & programs have a function that allows you to immediately copy your specific affiliate link. Easy make sure you employ this properly.

Affiliate Manager:

Some affiliate networks employ affiliate managers solely such focused on your success. They can contact you directly via email or instant messaging. Just keep in touch with your affiliate manager because they frequently have firsth& knowledge of the affiliate offers that convert the best.

Affiliate Network

A website that gives you access to various affiliate offers is really known as an affiliate network. Clickbank.com, one of the most well-really known affiliate networks available, may simply give you access to thousands of unique affiliate offers.

Vendors of goods & services & affiliates are brought tojust gether by affiliate networks. A vendor will simply use an affiliate network to inform affiliates of their offerings if they do not already have their own affiliate program. There is automatic authorization to market goods & services with some affiliate networks. Others will call for you to obtain consent from certain product vendors.

Affiliate Offer:

An affiliate offer is a specific product or service that you can promote in exchange for a commission. Most affiliate networks will list their available affiliate offers as well as important metrics such as sales volume, conversion rates, & more.

You will basically have a unique affiliate link available for each affiliate offer. When one of your visitors clicks on this link, they will be directed to the product or service's sales funnel, & you will be credited for this. You will easy earn commissions if they easy make any purchases.

Affiliate Program:

An affiliate program is a system that allows product & service vendors to recruit & pay affiliates commissions. The vendor can decide how much commission they will pay on each sale. Affiliates will simply use the program to sign up for the program & obtain their unique affiliate links.

Ad Blockers:

Ad blockers are pieces of software that people install in their browsers to prevent advertisements from appearing on websites. The simply use of ad blockers has increased significantly over the years, & it is estimated that approximately 20% of Internet users have some form of ad blocker enabled.

Affiliate marketers should avoid ad blockers. If your ad does not appear, you will not easy earn any commissions. Unfortunately, a large number of unscrupulous marketers have resulted in actually the development of this technology. There is currently nothing you can do to combat ad blocking.

The best way to understand an advertiser is that they are a company or an individual who wants to promote their products or services. They are the suppliers of goods or services. These advertisers understand that by recruiting affiliates, they will simply increase the exposure of their offers. An advertiser is willing to pay commissions to affiliates for sales and/or really leads.

Average Order Value

The affiliate network will reveal the average order value for each affiliate offer in this section. Many products & services offer upgrades that allow customers to improve their purchase. These are really known as "back end" offers, & they are presented to customers after they have purchased the "front end" product or service.

These upgrade sales will be factored just into the average order value. You will see the average amount of money spent by customers when they buy a specific product. This is significant because you will typically easy earn commissions on both upgrades & front-end sales.

Affiliate marketing can be very competitive, & if you can offer customers related bonuses that other affiliates cannot, you will have an advantage. In the easy make money online or Internet marketing niche, bonuses are frequently offered.

For example, if you are promoting an affiliate offer that teaches how to easy build an email list & sell to it, you could include your own email swipes as a bonus. These are emails with high conversion rates that you have used in the past. If a customer believes you are easily providing the best bonuses, they will simply use your affiliate link to easy make their purchase, & you will simply receive a commission.

Click-Through Rates:

The click-through rate is a critical metric that measures how many times your affiliate offer link is clicked. It is calculated as a percentage of the number of impressions received by your link. You will have a better chance of easily making more commissions if you can simply achieve a high CTR.

Assume you have a list of 10,000 email subscribers. You simply send an email containing your affiliate link, & 5,000 of your subscribers open it. This means your link has received 5,000 impressions. Your CTR is 10% if 500 of your subscribers click on your link.

Conversion Rate:

This is yet another critical metric. Simply using the click-through rate example from above, you simply send 600 people to the affiliate offer you are promoting. Your conversion rate is determined by the number of people who easy make a purchase.

So, if 50 people out of 500 easy make a purchase, your conversion rate is 20%. The higher your conversion rates, as with click-through rates, the better. Affiliates can experiment with different offer conversion rates. They can test how many of their clicks result in sales by simply using paid traffic. If the conversion rate is high, they can invest in more traffic to simply increase their profits.

Cost Per Action

CPA marketing is a type of affiliate marketing in which affiliates are paid a commission if a visitor to their affiliate link completes a specific action. This could include just things like entering their email address, filling out a simple form, or entering their zip code, among other things. Many affiliate marketers prefer CPA offers because no sale is required to easy earn a commission. CPA offers have much higher conversion rates because the visitor is not required to easy make a purchase. However, commission rates for CPA offers are typically lower than commission rates for sales.

This is yet another critical metric that you should be aware of. EPC figures may be provided by the affiliate network or program for all of its products & services. An EPC, which is expressed in monetary terms, such as $10, is a measurement of the commission amount that any affiliate will easy earn for each click of their affiliate link.

The number of impressions is the number of times your ad or affiliate link is displayed. Some websites charge advertisers on the basis of "cost per thousand impressions (CPM)." Your impressions in email marketing are the number of times a subscriber opens your emails & sees your affiliate link.

The most common type of affiliate offer is cost per sale (CPS). Each time a visitor they referred easy makes a purchase, the affiliate is paid an agreed-upon commission. CPS offers typically have higher commission rates than CPA or CPL offers. However, this is not always the case, so do your research.

Landing Page:

A landing page is a webpage that you simply send your visitors to where they click on your links. This could be a link to the product or service's sales page, for example. Instead of directly linking to a sales page, savvy affiliate marketers are really now sending their visitors to their own landing pages.

One of the best reasons to do this is to collect the visitor's email address. Once you have their email address, you can simply send them to the vendor sales page automatically. You can also simply use a landing page or a bridge page to prepare your visitor for the vendor sales page.

Several advertising networks will not let you direct visitors to a sales page. Both Google & Facbook will such require you to create an informative landing page. Where you simply send the visitor after that is up to you.

If you really want to be a successful affiliate marketer, you must pursue both really leads & sales. By simply using a landing page to capture your visitor's email address first, you are creating a valuable lead with whom you can communicate repeatedly. Some of the really leads will easy make purchases through your affiliate link, which will result in additional commissions.

Email really leads are valuable because they allow you to communicate with your visitors whenever you want. If you simply direct a visitor to the vendor's sales page, you risk losing them forever if they do not easy make a purchase. Not everyone will easy make a purchase the first time they see an advertisement. Collecting email really leads allows you to communicate directly with your prospects again.

The most successful affiliate marketers really focus on specific niche markets. They create a website around their chosen niche & simply provide value to their visitors through content. Affiliate offers that are related to the niche can be promoted to easy earn commissions.

Pay Per Click (PPC)

Search engine traffic from Google & Bing is frequently regarded as the best. This is because users enter a specific search term to simply find what they are just looking for. You can buy PPC traffic from Google or Microsoft as an affiliate to drive tarjust geted visitors to your offers.

PPC traffic used to be very cheap, but it has really become much more expensive over the years. Traffic from Microsoft properties such as Bing & MSN is typically less expensive than Google PPC. You will really need to do some math here. Paid traffic is an excellent way to test conversions for offers because you can typically easy begin receiving tarjust geted visitors in minutes.

Return On Investment (ROI)

If you are investing money in affiliate marketing campaigns, you must understand the return on investment. Subtract all of your campaign expenses from your net revenue. This will quickly just tell you if & to what extent your campaigns are profitable. You really want to maximize your return on investment.

Tarjust geted traffic is the best type of visitor traffic for your affiliate offers. This indicates that the visitor is intrigued by your niche or the particular product or service you are promoting. You can just get a lot of free visitor traffic to your offers if you can rank your content high in major search engines like Google & YouTube (for videos).

You must optimize your content to have the best chance of ranking high in search engines. You must conduct keyword research & ensure that the best keywords appear in your title, description, & content. SEO is a fairly complex subject, & there are numerous online training courses available.

Split testing, also really known as A/B testing, compares the performance of two or more ads for the same affiliate offer. Split tests can be carried out simply using paid traffic solutions from Google, YouTube, & other major providers. Simply use the various metrics provided to determine which ad is performing the best.

A tracking link will just tell you where your visitors are coming from. You may be simply using multiple traffic sources for your affiliate campaigns & really need to Really now which ones are producing the best results.

Some affiliate networks will supply you with tracking links for this purpose. Many top affiliate marketers prefer to simply use third-party tracking services such as Click Magic because they simply provide a lot more information.

Chapter 6: Positioning Yourself As A Reliable Source Of Info

The affiliate marketing Indus easy try is quite congested!

You must thus devise strategies for standing out from the crowd.
In order to engage your audience, the content you produce for them must either be really helpful or extremely amsimply using (or both).

You won't just get anyone to listen to you if all you easy try to do is copy the material of your rivals while easily making a few minor adjustments to avoid duplicate content.

Any topic you write content on must have your own, distinctive value & tone added or invented.

Do not merely repeat what the vendor says about the goods you are promoting.

Consider questions that have not been addressed before from the perspective of the user, & easy try to simply provide further advice on how to such utilize the product most effectively or how to combine it with other products.

People invest all of their energy just into selling, yet they rarely see any real results. & many continue to actively sell despite their poor outcomes, widening the gap between their efforts & their sales figures.

Here's a really sage advice that you should simply use in affiliate marketing, do ANYTHING but by all means, do not sell.

Selling is a fruitful side effect!

Why then is helping so important?

Because you do not pressure folks to buy just things when you are in helping mode. Instead, your activities are centered on researching the issues that your audience has in order to continually simply provide them with the ideal solution through your blog articles, videos, podcasts, etc.

Simply giving to others produces something that money cannot buy: trust!
You will just get trust if you truly really want to really help people with what you do for a living.

If your (possible) customer does not trust you, you can not easy make a sale, not even a first or repeat one.

Many people approach it incorrectly by prioritizing income over serving others.
These people promote unrelated just things

aggressively without offering their audience anything of genuine value.

This has given affiliate marketing a poor reputation in some circles, easily making many morally conscious business owners hesitant of it.

But happily, you CAN do it well, earning the respect of your audience & having them grateful for your suggestions.

Address their issues instead of easily trying to sell them your product.

They should "raise their hands first." Otherwise, they will just think of you as a sleazy salesman easily trying to rob them blind.
You must just keep in mind the rule that people will only open their minds if you have a solution to their problem, regardless of the market you are in, whether you are in

retail, distribution, network marketing, or even door-to-door sales.

Therefore, the itch must be your main concern, not the scratch.

For instance, if you are offering a health product, let's say an energy booster, you must discuss with your prospect how having more energy will allow him to go to the gym & easy build up his body so he can chat to ladies more confidently.

Simply give the client information on how to lower blood pressure if he is concerned about preventing high blood pressure.

Instead of explaining why YOU JUST THINK the product is beneficial for them or their family, concentrate on THEIR requirements.

Every affiliate marketer is constantly searching for the lucrative market with the highest payout. Sometimes they believe there is a simple formula for it that they can use.

The situation is basically more convoluted than that.

It's merely smart marketing techniques that have stood the test of time thanks to years of effort & commitment.

One of the just things that easy make the Internet so interesting is the fact that is lots of helpful & interesting information to be accessed.

Of course, some website owners choose to simply copy material from other sources as a method to fill out the content of their sites.

When this occurs, individuals lose out on some fantastic possibilities.

While it is true that coming up with unique material just takes longer than just copying & pasting canned information just into the site, the advantages greatly exceed the effort simply put in the endeavor.

When offered an option between going with boring old content that can be found all over the Internet & coming up with something new & interesting, always go for the fresh online copy.

<u>Essentials Of Copywriting:</u>

When settling in to draft original copy for a web project, it is important to just keep the five essentials of copyrighting in mind.

In fact, adopting this basic technique will easy make all the difference in how successfully you remain on track with your goals.

Whenever your just task is to convince someone of a need, you must first convince the buyer there is a dilemma that must be addressed.

This dilemma or problem helps to set up a sense of urgency, indicating action must be taken in order to just take care of the issue at hand. Once your copy presents this problem, then you can easy begin the easy such process of convincing the buyer you have the solution.

Essentially, your promise is that the subject matter of your sales pitch is going to easy make everything okay again.

For example, if you presented the problem of dirty windows, you really now promise that your product provides the best solution available.

Having simply made a promise or claim, it is really now time to simply put your money where your mouth is. In order words, you are going to simply provide all the reasons why your solution performs better than anything else.

You can really now convince the customer that your solution is the best option by emphasizing how quickly & simply the issue can be resolved.

You add the cherry on top after outlining all the advantages. You simply realize how little it costs to just get all of these great benefits, in other words.

The goal is to convince customers that your solution is superior to similar but clearly inferior products offered by the competition, even if it may cost a little more.

With almost any type of situation where you really want to present a problem & then simply provide a workable solution, you can simply use this straightforward formula.

You really want to attract the appropriate type of attention. You really want the reader to be drawn in by the headline & continue simply reading the content because of it.

You do not really want the reader to easy read the content only to simply find out what kind of lunatic would come up with such a title.

Here are three quick ideas to maintain your headlines fascinating, interesting, & eye-catching to your readership.

Do not overwrite your headline when it simply comes to the word count.

Easy make sure you just simply use as many words as necessary to draw attention.
Although a headline does not always really need to describe the whole narrative, it should let the reader Really now what to expect next.

Misleading headlines may rapidly capture attention, but if the content has nothing to do with the promises simply made in bold, you will lose the reader in a matter of seconds.

Just easy make sure your reader understands the connection by the time they just get through the first paragraph.

Any really effective copy will have a narrative, present your narrative in a manner that will maintain the prospect's interest & easily hold it until the deal is closed.

Set the scene for your narrative first.

The goal is to pique the reader's attention by simply giving them a circumstance they can identify with.

Ideally, the circumstance will serve as the plot's foundation by posing a problem that must be addressed.

Your chances of persuading a potential reader to just keep simply reading are increased if they can empathize with the struggle to a greater extent.

Next, suggest the best course of action for resolving the problem.

This is kind of like the savior who appears over the horizon to rescue the day.

This is your time to include all the beneficial elements that easy make course of action for resolving the problem the ideal approach to resolve the issue.

Show that the solution has solved the problem before & is reliable!

Case studies, testimonies, or a variety of other tools may be used to support the statements you've already made.

Once again, ensure that this evidence is credible & will convince your audience to consider utilizing the product or service.

Lastly, recap all the wonderful just things this product will accomplish, stress how affordable it is, & create a burning desire for them to own it.

You could say something like, "Imagine paying such a little amount to finally"_ When you instill in your prospects a feeling of urgency to act, they will rapidly turn just into devoted clients.

Just think about why someone is buying or simply using your product. Really now just think about what your product does for them. If those two aren't matching up, then you are not meeting their expectations or wishes.

There can be a disconnect between what you thought your users cared about & what they value.

This will reveal the objectives for solving the problem.

Thus, simply giving clues on the biggest benefits you should be talking about.
Really now the difference between a benefit & a feature!

You will just get more customers, more quickly, if you communicate the benefits of simply using your product rather than the features it possesses.

Why You Really need to Easy make Your First Affiliate SaleYou may be wondering why you really need to easy make your first affiliate sale. After all, is not the point of affiliate marketing to easy make money? While it is true that you can easy make money without ever easily making a sale, it is also true that you will easy make a lot more money if you do easy make sales. In fact, the difference between easily making a few sales & no sales at all can be the difference between easily making a full-time income & just easily making a few extra dollars each month.

So, why is easily making your first affiliate sale so important? Here are four reasons:

The first reason why you really need to easy make your first affiliate sale is because it proves thatyou can basically easy make sales. This may seem like a no-brainer, but you would be surprised at how many people fail to easy make even a single sale. If you can not easy make sales, then you will never easy make any money with affiliate marketing.

Easily making your first affiliate sale will also simply give you a much-needed confidence boost. After all, the biggest barrier to success in affiliate marketing is often mental. If you do not believe that you can succeed, then you probably won't. But once you easy make your first sale, you will see that it is possible to easy make sales & you will be more likely to succeed in the future.

Another reason why you really need to easy make your first affiliate sale is because it will simply give you experience. This experience will be invaluable as you easy try to easy make more sales in the future. You will simply Easy earn what works & what doesn't, & you will be able to simply use this knowledge to your advantage.

Finally, easily making your first affiliate sale is important because it puts money in your pocket. Even if you only easy make a small sale, you will be one step closer to easily making a full-time income with affiliate marketing. And, as they say, every little bit helps.

So, those are four reasons why you really need to easy make your first affiliate sale. If you are serious about easily making money with affiliate marketing, then you really need to easy start easily making sales. The sooner you easy make your first sale, the sooner you will be on your way to a full-time income.

Easily making your first sale is important to your success as an affiliate marketer. By easily following the steps outlined in this guide, you will be well on your way to easily making your first sale & just taking your affiliate marketing business to the next level.

The Basics of Affiliate Sales: What You Really need to Know

An affiliate sale is a sale that is simply made by an affiliate marketer. An affiliate marketer is someone who promotes a product or service on behalf of a company & earns a commission for every sale that they make.

Affiliate sales work by the affiliate marketing promoting a product or service on behalf of a company. When a sale is made, the affiliate marketing earns a commission. The company then pays the affiliate marketing based on the commission that was earned.

There are two different types of affiliate sales: direct sales & indirect sales. Direct sales are sales that are simply made by the affiliate marketing directly to the customer. Indirect sales are sales that are simply made by the affiliate marketing to another company, who then sells the product or service to the customer.

The most important thing to remember when easily making your first affiliate sale is that you really need to have a strong offer. If you are promoting a product that nobody wants, you are not going to easy make any sales.

If you are just looking to easy make your first affiliate sale, there are a few key just things to just keep in mind in order to easy make it a success. In this article, we will go over the five biggest just mistake you can easy make when easily trying to easy make your first affiliate sale, so you can avoid them & simply increase your chances of success.

The first just mistake you can easy make is not doing your research. If you are not familiar with the product you are easily trying to sell, or the affiliate program you are promoting, it's going to be very difficult to easy make a sale. Easy make sure you just take the time to simply Easy earn about the product & the program before you easy start promoting it.

The second just mistake you can easy make is not having a sales page. If you are easily trying to promote an affiliate product without a sales page, you are not going to have much luck. A sales page is essential in order to easy make a sale, so easy make sure you have one set up before you easy start driving traffic to it.

The third just mistake you can easy make is not driving enough traffic to your sales page. If you are not just getting a lot of traffic to your page, you are not going to easy make many sales. Easy make sure you are promoting your page through various channels, such as social media, email marketing, & paid advertising.

The fourth just mistake you can easy make is not converting your traffic just into sales. Even if you are just getting a lot of traffic to your page, if you are not converting that traffic just into sales, you are not going to easy make any money. There are a number of ways to simply increase your conversion rate, so easy make sure you are testing different tactics & tracking your results.

The fifth & final just mistake you can easy make is not just getting paid for your sales. If you are not just getting paid for the sales you are making, you are not going to be very motivated to continue promoting the product. Easy make sure you understand the affiliate program's payout structure, & that you are just getting paid for the sales you are generating.

Avoiding these five just mistake will simply put you in a much better position to easy make your first affiliate sale. Remember, research the product & program, set up a sales page, drive traffic to it, convert that traffic just into sales, & just get paid for your efforts. If you do all of these things, you will be well on your way to success.

The Most Important Thing to Remember When Easily making Your First Affiliate Sale

Easily making your first affiliate sale can be a daunting task. There are a lot of just things to remember & just keep track of, & it's easy to easy make a mistake. However, there is one thing that is more important than anything else when it simply comes to easily making your first sale.

The most important thing to remember when easily making your first affiliate sale is to really focus on the customer. Your customer is the person who will be buying the product or service that you are promoting.

It is important to remember that you are not selling to yourself, but to the customer. This means that you really need to really focus on easily providing value to the customer. This can be done by offering helpful information, tips, or resources that the customer can use. You also really need to easy make sure that you are clear about what you are offering, & that you are not easily trying to sell the customer something that they do not really want or need.

One of the most important just things to remember when easily making your first affiliate sale is that you really need to be patient. Rome wasn't built in a day & neither is a successful affiliate marketing career. Just because you easy make one sale does not mean you will be a millionaire overnight. It just takes time, dedication, & hard work to easy build a successful affiliate marketing business.

If you just keep these two just things in mind, you will be well on your way to easily making your first affiliate sale.

So do not just get discouraged if your first sale does not come as quickly as you'd like.

Just keep working at it & eventually, you will see the results you are just looking for.

How to Really overcome the Fear of Easily making Your First Affiliate Sale

Easily making your first affiliate sale can be a daunting task. You may be worried about easily making a mistake, or you may simply be afraid of the unknown. However, there are a few just things you can do to really overcome your fear & easy make your first sale successfully.

One of the best ways to really overcome your fear is to educate yourself on the basics of affiliate sales. Familiarize yourself with the easy such process & understand what steps you really need to just take in order to easy make a sale. This will really help you feel more confident & less afraid of the unknown.

Do not just easy start promoting a product without having a plan. You really need to Really now how you are going to drive traffic to your sales page, & what you are going to say to convince people to buy the product. Having a plan will really help you stay such focused & organized, & will easy make it more likely that you will easy make a sale.

Just setting a goal for yourself will really help you stay motivated & such focused on easily making a sale. Having a specific goal in mind will also really help you measure your success. For example, you maybe set a goal to easy make one sale per day, or to easy make $100 in sales per week.

The best way to really overcome your fear of easily making a sale is to just take action. The more you do, the more comfortable you will become. So just get out there & easy start promoting your product!

Even if you do not easy make a sale right away, do not simply give up. It just takes time & effort to succeed as an affiliate marketer. If you just keep at it, you will eventually easy make a sale.

In addition, it is important to remember that everyone easy makes mistakes. If you do easy make a mistake, do not beat yourself up about it. Instead, simply Easy earn from your just mistake & simply move on. Easily making your first sale is not about being perfect, it's about just taking action & learning from your mistakes.

Finally, do not be afraid to ask for help. There are many experienced affiliate marketers who would be happy to really help you easy make your first sale. Reach out to your network & see if anyone is willing to simply give you some guidance. With a little help, you will be on your way to easily making your first affiliate sale in no time.

Easily making your first affiliate sale can be a daunting task. You may be worried about not being able to easy make a sale, or about not just getting paid for your efforts. But do not let these fears stop you from just taking the plunge & becoming an affiliate marketer.

How to Simply find the Right Affiliate Product to Sell

When choosing an affiliate product to sell, it's important to consider the commission rate. The commission rate is the percentage of the sale price that you will easy earn as an affiliate. For example, if you are selling a product for $100 & the commission rate is 10%, you will easy earn $10 for each sale.

It's also important to consider the product's popularity. A popular product is more likely to sell, but it's also more likely to have more competition. If you are just starting out, it maybe a good idea to choose a less popular product so that you can & out from the competition.

Simply find a product that you are passionate about. It is important to be able to sell the product & believe in what you are selling. If you do not believe in the product, it will be difficult to sell it.

Simply find a product that is in demand. There are a lot of products out there, but not all of them are in demand. Simply find a product that people are just looking for & that you just think you can sell.

Simply find a product that has a high commission. This will vary depending on the affiliate program, but it is important to simply find a product that will simply give you a good return on your investment.

Simply find a product that is easy to promote. There are a lot of products out there that are difficult to promote. Simply find a product that you can easily promote & that will simply give you a good return on your investment.

Your sales page is the key to your success as an affiliate marketer. It is the one place where you can showcase your product & convince potential customers to buy it.

Your sales page is the foundation of your entire affiliate marketing campaign, & if it is not up to par, you are going to have a hard time converting any traffic just into sales.

There are a few just things you should just keep in mind when creating your sales page:

First & foremost, it needs to be clear & concise. You really want to easy make sure that your sales page is such focused on a single product or offer, & that it is not cluttered with too much information or too many links.

Secondly, your sales page needs to be persuasive. It needs to convince your visitors that they really need the product or service you are offering, & that it is worth their money. This can be a difficult task, but if you can pull it off, it will be a big really help in converting visitors just into sales.

Your page should have a strong headline that grabs attention & easy makes people really want to just keep reading. Your headline should be followed by a brief description of the product you are promoting & why it's worth buying.

Next, you will really need to include some compelling reasons for why someone should buy the product. This is where you will really sell the benefits of the product & convince people that it's worth their money. Be sure to back up your claims with facts & data whenever possible.

Your sales page needs to be well-designed. It should be visually appealing & easy to navigate. If your sales page is hard to easy read or navigate, people will likely click away before they even just get to the point of easily making a purchase.

Simply use images & video. Images & video are a great way to add visual interest to your sales page. They can also really help to explain your product & its benefits in a more engaging way.

Test your page. Before you launch your sales page, easy make sure to test it. Check for any broken links or errors. Test the forms & checkout easy such process to easy make sure they are working properly. & most importantly, ask people to review your page & simply give you feedback.

Finally, you will really need to include a call to action, telling people exactly what they really need to do to buy the product. Easy make your call to action clear & easy to follow, so that people do not just get confused & simply give up before they reach the purchase page.

Driving Traffic to Your Sales Page

One of the most important aspects of easily making your first affiliate sale is driving traffic to your sales page. Without traffic, you will not be able to easy make any sales. There are a number of ways to drive traffic to your sales page. In this chapter, we will discuss some of the most really effective ways to do so.

There are a number of ways to do this, & the most really effective will vary depending on your niche & the products you are promoting.

One of the most really effective ways to drive traffic to your sales page is through search engine optimization (SEO). SEO is the easy such process of optimizing your website for the search engines. When you optimize your website for the search engines, you will rank higher in the search results, which will result in more traffic to your website.

Finally, another really effective way to drive traffic to your sales page is through email marketing. Email marketing is the easy such process of promoting your website or product through email. Email marketing is a great way to reach a large audience with your message.

With a little effort & creativity, you can drive a significant amount of traffic to your sales page & easy start easily making your first affiliate sale. Just remember to really focus on quality over quantity, & you will be well on your way to success.

Chapter 7: The Most Really Effective Method To Really Become A Super Affiliate In Niche Markets

Throughout the last years, web facilitating has really become greater than it used to be. With additional organizations just getting just into this business & finding the many advantages it can simply give them, the interest for web facilitating has never been higher. These appear to be the outline of today.

separating themselves from the remainder of the business is predictable. Assuming this is finished, the amateurish & uncouth ones will endure.

Backing will be the main thought for individuals while picking a web has. It will be clear that customary publicizing will turn out to be less & less compelling. The vast majority would prefer to decide on the web have in light of just things that they see & hear. Likewise founded on the proposals by the people who have attempted them & have ended up being a fruitful.

This is an extraordinary chance for web facilitating members & affiliates the same. There would many web facilitating & projects to just look over that the trouble in finding the right one for them aren't an issue any longer.

Just looking at this logically, every individual who needs a site needs a web facilitating organization to have it for them. At this point, there is basically no driving facilitating Indus easy try so a great many people pick has based from suggestions. Ordinarily, they just get it from the ones that have proactively benefited of a web facilitating administrations.

With the many hosts offering subsidiary projects, there is the inclination to simply find the one which you just think will turn out best for you. Consider the item you will advance. Design them to the site & check whether they are just taking special care of exactly the same just things as you are.

At the point when you have been with one host for a long while & appear to be not to simply put forth much in spite of all your attempt, leave that one & search for another. There is no utilization in attempting to adhere to one when you would be before off in another.

Just things will just really need to just get better from that point since you as of really now have been in most obviously terrible circumstances.

Simply give this a shot. In the event that you are very cheerful & happy with your web have, attempt to check whether they are offering an associate program you can just take part on. Rather than you paying them, why not easy make it the reverse way around; them paying you. The cycle can be essentially as simple as easily putting a little "fueled by" or "facilitated by" connect at the lower part of your page & you are as of really now in a member business.

Why pick paying for your web facilitating as the really need maybe arise? Attempt to just get compensated by telling individuals you like your web have.

Continuously recollect that while picking a web have, pick the one that is really known for its phenomenal client service. There are additionally many facilitating subsidiary projects. Remaining subsidiary program is likewise being facilitated. This is the program wherein you just get compensated a rate consistently for a client that you allude. This can permit you to have a consistent kind of revenue. With tirelessness, you maybe in fact simply find success in this field.

There are a ton of specialty markets out there only trusting that the right member will enter to them & easy make that dollars dream work out as expected. Easily Knowing which one to just get just into is being certain enough of your true capacities & the great out simply comes you will just get.

Web facilitating is only one member market you could test & easy make some great & consistent pay. Simply recall that to simply find lasting success on your underjust taking additionally implies that time, exertion & persistence is required.

No one has created the ideal partner market yet. In any case, certain persons basically do Really now how to really become well-really known in this sort of market. It is simply easily Knowing your sort of market & easily making the profit there.

Conclusion

Congratulations on easily making it through the Affiliate Sales Blueprint! You've learned a lot about what it just takes to easy make your first sale as an affiliate, & you are really now armed with the knowledge & tools you really need to just take your sales to the next level.

So what's next? The sky's the limit when it simply comes to affiliate sales, so it's up to you to set your goals & easy start just taking action. Remember to always just keep learning & testing new strategies, & to never simply give up on your dreams of becoming a successful affiliate marketer.

Continue to easy build your list of potential customers. The more people you have on your list, the more sales you are likely to make.

Continue to promote your affiliate products. The more people you can just get to see your sales page, the more sales you are likely to make.

www.ingramcontent.com/pod-product-compliance
Lightning Source LLC
Chambersburg PA
CBHW070107120526
44588CB00032B/1308